This is Bill.

Bill sees a hill.

Bill will skip up a hill.

Skip, skip, skip!

See the drip?

Will Bill slip?

Oh, a rip!

See the dip?

Will Bill trip?

Oh, his lip!

See the tip?

Will Bill flip?

Oh, his hip!

Bill is ill.

He sees his hill.

Will Bill skip up the hill?